Beekeeping:

Beginners Guide to Starting your First DIY Backyard Bee Colony. Simple, Easy and Fast Step-by-Step Instructions to Homemade Organic Honey

By Michael Moore

Copyright © 2016 Michael Moore

All rights reserved.

This eBook is geared towards providing exact and reliable information in regards to the topic and issue covered. The publication is sold on the idea that the publisher is not required to render an accounting, or otherwise, qualified services. If advice is necessary, legal or professional, a practiced individual in the profession should be ordered.

In no way is it legal to reproduce, duplicate, or transmit any part of this document by either electronic means or in printed format. Recording of this publication is strictly prohibited and any storage of this document is not allowed unless with written permission from the publisher. All rights reserved.

The information provided herein is stated to be truthful and consistent, in that any liability, in terms of inattention or otherwise, by any usage or abuse of any policies, processes, or directions contained within is the solitary and utter responsibility of the recipient reader. Under no circumstances will any legal responsibility or blame be held against the publisher for any reparation, damages, or monetary loss due to the information herein, either directly or indirectly.

Respective authors own all copyrights not held by the

ISBN:10:1537734601
ISBN-13:9781537734606

CONTENTS

	INTRODUCTION	i
1	THE IMPORTANCE OF BEEKEEPING TODAY	1
2	THE BASICS OF A BEE COLONY	15
3	CHOOSING THE RIGHT BEE FOR YOU	25
4	THE BEEHIVE	31
5	GETTING YOUR BEES INTO THE HIVE	40
6	MAINTAINING YOUR COLONY & HIVE	53
7	HOW TO AVOID & SOLVE COMMON PROBLEMS	68
8	CONCLUSION	74

INTRODUCTION

A beehive in your garden can make a big difference in the life of a gardener or farmer of any skill level. You can consider doing some beekeeping, if you are doing some gardening in your background; especially if you have enough space for it. Bees can help you do so much for your garden. They can help you produce larger and bigger fruits, vegetables, and flowers.

Generally, beekeeping is considered a minor industry, but because of it being beneficial to our ecology, specifically to agriculture; beekeeping is becoming more than essential and valuable to human life as pollination is an essential step to keeping our ecosystem balanced.

Commodities derived from bee products such as honey and beeswax are increasing in demand as new health benefits are revealed and with its use and application. Whether you want to learn more about beekeeping for the benefits of enjoying it as a hobby or for extra money earning potential, learning about this interesting insect is something worth exploring.

This book is designed to guide you through a do-it-yourself backyard beekeeping while providing you with a full understanding of **the basics of beekeeping**—understanding all about honey bee biology and colonies, learning how to get started, managing a hive, helping you pick the right set up and eventually raising a successful beekeeper out of you while you manage colonies both for fun and profit.

Beekeeping: Beginners Guide to Starting your First DIY Backyard Bee Colony. Simple, Easy and Fast Step by Step Instructions to Homemade Organic Honey aims to thoroughly equip you with the skills and knowledge essential to the trade for the best results. This book aims to provide you with the basics needed so you will be able to have a high yield of honey produced by healthy bees while they pollinate your garden or nearby greenery.

MICHAEL MOORE

THE IMPORTANCE OF BEEKEEPING TODAY

As Colony Collapse Disorder (CCD) is getting to be a hot issue among gardeners and beekeepers today, there is an absolute need to do something about our beekeeping industry as it does not only affect them but all mankind. CCD is a phenomenon where the hive experiences a sudden loss of worker bees. The worker bees leave the queen with food and a few nurse bees to tend to larva. This sudden loss of bees in the colony results is massive economic and ecological damage, with agricultural industries find a direct correlation to decreased harvesting yields.

The actual reason behind CCD is not agreed among the scientific community. However, this book will provide you sound advice on how best to prevent the occurrence. Just as Albert Einstein once implied that the disappearance of bees will have a drastic effect on the life here on earth, we need to be more concerned with our bees and natural habitat. This is the reason why we are encouraging you on your beekeeping pursuit through this beekeeping for beginners DIY guide.

Honeybees are vital to the production of our fresh food produce, which include, a large amount of our most commonly consumed fruits and vegetables, because bees are responsible for pollination, we owe them a lot for everything that we lay on our tables. The lack of adequate pollination can result in low yields and agricultural produce that are either small or in bad shape.

Many agricultural producers underestimate their need for pollination. This could be the reason why there is an inadequate harvest. Unluckily, there is no substitute for natural pollination provided by bees and butterflies. Hence, for crops that need insect pollination, a large number of bees must be around to be able to produce a commercial quantity.

Pollination can be one major industry that our government sector must look into. Pollination as a business opportunity offers you with additional benefits from making money out of beekeeping. Though, of course, adequate security measures must be provided while having your bees for hire. Beekeepers who can produce a good crop of honey and also rent their bees for crop pollination can build more than adequate security in their business, especially during the times when the honey crop fails.

Honeybees are usually needed in pollination of high bush blueberries, cranberries, raspberries, and blackberries. Cucurbit crops like cucumbers, squash, pumpkins, watermelons, and muskmelons or cantaloupes need to be pollinated for commercial production as many plants cannot be pollinated in any other way.

Benefits to Gardeners and Organic Gardens

Bees need our help just as we need them. They are perfect pollinators, alongside butterflies and hummingbirds. Their part in the eco-system is critical, but they are most often misunderstood. People always think of bees as aggressive buzzing insects that are ready to sting at anything near. This is actually far from the truth, as like most living beings in the world; bees do not sting unless provoked.

According to statistics in the US, bees are pollinating 80 percent of the flowering plants and 75 percent of fruits, vegetables, and nuts. The presence of bees in your garden will definitely increase you're the chances of your flowers blooming beautifully. Native flowers like daisies, asters, and sunflowers are well-loved by bees and butterflies. These flowers easily attract them.

Pollinators depend on these flowering plants that bloom from spring through summer and fall. You don't need a large garden to feed these insects. Even just a single flower pot or a window flower box will help restore a part of the habitat that has been compromised due to development. Stop seeing these insects as aggressive and dangerous. Instead, take the time to think of them as wonderful creatures in wildlife. They are here to help and we should also think of ways to help them back and save our ecological system as well.

Now that we know how important these bees are to our food chain, beekeeping needs to be encouraged. We need to help our bees by helping them live a natural productive life even in the safety of your own backyards. Of course, this is only applicable to those with large backyards, especially in the countryside. However, you need to consider the kind of law that exist in your state or country where you are living regarding beekeeping. Urban beekeeping is also a possibility when done correctly, but the size of your colony as well as the type of bee hive used will defer slightly depending on your surrounding environment. Don't forget to leave a review if you've found this book helpful.

Types of Honey

Honey bees make honey from the nectar of plants. They sip on the moisture and add enzymes to give honey its unique taste. Bees store the honey in the cells of their comb, when the moisture content of honey is about 17 percent they secure their honey by sealing the cells with white beeswax capping.

Bees have the ability to blend honey naturally by combining pollens from different flowers in an area where no one flower predominates. When bees have access to larger areas with only one kind of flower like clover, buckwheat, goldenrod, or basswood, they produce honey with a flavour typical of that particular flowering plant. Remember, however, that honey is also blended during commercial selling to create a specific taste.

In fact, cheap mass produced honey commonly found in the supermarket shelf is mostly not real honey but a concoction of cheap sugars and flavouring.

Honey is classified by the type of food source the bees use, the type of flowers used by the bees as well as the colour and consistency, it can also be classified by the process used during the manufacturing period. There are more than 300 different varieties of honey and each variety has its own texture, color, taste, and flavor depending upon the floral or regional source, and treatment used. Most people are only aware of honey in their liquid or set form. Others manage to dig deeper to explore on the taste. Here are some types of honey one can come across with either in their local areas or commodity stores. We chose some of the basic ones to go over, so you understand enough about the ones that are easily found, available and the types that you yourself will be harvesting soon.

By the Food Source:

Blossom Honey

This is the nectar honey which comes either from flower nectarines or nectar, that sweet substance secreted by plants glands.

Blossom honey is what most people, if not all people imagine honey is, however you will quickly learn that bees do not just use nectar to make honey.

Honeydew Honey

This kind of honey is referred to as forest honey and it comes from the excretions of insects that feed on the sap of a plant. It is normally dark in color and very strong in flavor. This honey is also known as tree honey, oak honey, pine honey, fir honey, forest honey, and so on. It is rich in minerals.

However, honeydew honey cam cause complications to the health of a bee colony as the sap normally includes many elements the bees are unable to digest properly and lack the protein floral nectar naturally provides. Novice beekeepers are not advised to place their bee colony where plant sap is the predominant food resource for the bees.

Certified Organic Honey

Organic honey is free from the effects of pesticides and antibiotics, being obtained from floral sources that are free from chemicals, air pollutions, and other industrial pollutants. You must be aware that not all organic honey is certified. Only those that are certified by well-known organizations and bodies are considered certified Organic Honey. Before a honey can be certified, the land used by the bees to collect and make honey needs to also be subjected to strict guidance to the land as also being organic.

By the Flower Source:

Mono-Floral and Poly-Floral

Mono-floral honey comes from one single variety of flower but it does not mean that this honey does not contain anything from other floral varieties. In fact, it may contain a small percentage of various flowers while a large portion of it comes from a single floral type. Honey lovers and beekeepers sometimes prefer mono-floral over other types.

Poly-floral, on the other hand, is the complete opposite of the mono-floral. It comes from many different kinds flowers and can also be known as wildflower honey. If the place you live is like most, then your bees are most likely going to produce poly-floral honey. However, if you wish to produce mono-floral honey, then simply plant more of your desired type of floral source within the immediate surrounding area. Bees, like all animals travel the path of least resistant and will collect the nectar of the nearby plants first before venturing further.

By Texture and Consistency:

Comb Honey

This type comes directly from the honeycombs made by bees from beeswax. This is the most original and unfiltered type of honey but the most expensive. People love it when honey is in its most natural state. Since this type of honey is pure and does not undergo any kind of treatment or heating. Some people enjoy eating both the honey and the comb.

Cut Comb Honey

This is the kind of liquid honey you may find in a jar and is actually a combination of liquid honey and comb. Honeycombs are cut in pieces and edges along with the pieces are packed in individual jars. This is pure honey in its natural state with no processing or heating involved except cutting and packaging. There are some sellers who would use acacia honey as the base being liquid and arrange the comb to float on top.

Liquid Honey

This is the most common form, which is extracted from the comb by straining. This is used essentially for baking, cooking, and sweeteners for beverages. It can also be used as a spread on toasts or bread.

Most honey sold in health food stores is liquid honey.

Liquid honey can be filtered, ultra-filtered, or even left unfiltered. When unfiltered, it carried residues of beeswax, propolis, and pollen. Some are filtered to make it appear clearer. A commercial grade of this liquid honey is ultra-filtered, heated and processed for a better appearance during packaging.

Set Honey

In contrast to liquid honey, this refers to the solid or thicker type of honey. It is also liquid at the start but soon turns into granules after a short period of time. If it becomes too hard, you can soften it by placing the jar in warm water.

It is also called creamed honey and colour varies according to the floral source, but is mostly opaque with various hues of yellow. This is usually used as a spread and has to undergo some processes to control crystallization. Though it still carries some small amount of crystals, it does not become thick or cloudy. Other names include honey fondant, churned honey, spun honey, and whipped honey.

By Manufacture Process used:

Pasteurized Honey

This type of honey is known as heated honey. Because it undergoes rigorous filtration and heating, the process dissolves the seed crystals and is unlikely to granulate over time. Supermarkets prefer pasteurized honey because it does not solidify, turns into granules or become cloudy even if stored for a long time or even when storing condition is not perfect. Sad to say, there's no health benefit to pasteurized honey.

Crystallized Honey

It is partially solid, granulated and crystallized. Natural crystallization is formed while stored and does not affect the quality of honey, though it appears thick and cloudy.

Raw Honey

This type of honey is real and extracted without undergoing any heating process beyond 48 degrees centigrade. It is not even filtered so you can still find some residues of wax, pollen, wings and legs in it. People love this type of honey and believe it to have anti-allergic properties. Also, this type of honey is more nutritious, higher in minerals, and carries a stronger flavor.

Ultra-filtered Honey

You can obtain this commercial grade honey by heating the honey beyond 48 degrees centigrade. Most commercial vendors also prefer this type because it is easy to mix with other food. When packed and bottled, it appears neat and clean. However, ultra-filtered honey loses its natural flavour and nutrients in the process. It is considered to be very low in quality by honey experts and not preferred to domestic or whole consumption.

THE BASICS OF A BEE COLONY

Honeybees are social insects and can't be solitary as they are engaged in a complex system made up of varied tasks and responsibilities. They live together in a large, well-organized colony. The behaviour of a colony as a whole has fascinated people for many years. Many of whom end up studying their amazing behavioral patterns. Behaviours like communication, nest building, ecological participation, defences, and distribution of labors are just some of the amazing facts humans have gathered about these fascinating insects.

Life Cycle of a Honeybee

There are four key stages in a life of a honeybee: Egg, larva, pupa, and adult. However, there can be some variations depending on the species (honeybee, bumblebee, and solitary bee etc) and the role of the bee in the colony. We will discuss in further detail of different roles within a bee colony and the characteristics of each type of bee.

Unlike the bumblebee, honeybee colonies can survive even during the winter as long as they have enough food, warmth, are free of diseases and safe from predators. Although they are usually fewer in number during this season with no drones present.

The queen and the rest of the colony form a cluster to survive the cold season. This is not a laying season for the queen bee, so there's no brood to tend to. However, as the warm season approaches and flowers start to bloom, bees start to get out of their hiding place and resume their normal work while the queen starts with the reproduction function.

After three days, eggs will be hatched into larvae. A single larva is fed about 1,300 times a day. Some worker bees are assigned to nurse these broods, and are referred to as brood nurses. These nurses give the larva their food made from pollen, honey and secretions called bee bread. Potential honeybee queens are given royal jelly, a highly nutritional mixture that contains many minerals and vitamins.

After 6 days, each larva spins itself a cocoon and turn into a pupa. It takes about 10 days for a worker bee, and slightly longer for drones while new queens take about 6 days to come out from pupae.

In a honeybee colony, you can find three kinds of adult bees: the queen bee, drones, and workers. All worker bees combine their efforts in nest building, brood rearing, and food collection and storage. Each one has its definite task to perform in relation to its adult stage. However, combined efforts of these three (queen, drones, and workers) are needed for survival and reproduction.

Labor activities are dependent on the age of the

worker bees and vary according to the needs of the colony. The strength of the colony and reproduction of honeybees depends largely on the reproduction capacity of the queen bee, which dictates the size of the workforce, and the amount of food produced and needed. As the colony grows in size, the more efficient it becomes. A colony can grow up to 600,000 workers.

The Queen

There is only one queen in every colony. Being the only sexually developed female, she is responsible for reproducing other bees, which constitute her colony. She can produce both fertilized and non-fertilized eggs and can lay a great number of eggs during spring and early summer. During the peak of her reproduction, the queen can lay as many as 1500 eggs per day. This quantity gradually declines in early October and totally stops by early next spring (January). A queen bee can produce up to 250,000 eggs per year and possibly over a million in her lifetime.

A queen bee is easily distinguished because of her

physical appearance, which is much longer than the drone and worker bee especially during her laying period. Her wings cover only about 2/3 of her abdomen while both drone and worker bees have wings that reach the tip of their abdomen when folded.

There are three major reasons for bees to raise a queen: Queenlessness, failing queen, and swarming. You can observe a slight difference in the appearance of each cell depending on the situation that occurs.

Queenlessness
It's very easy to determine if your colony has experienced queenlessness, by of course, not be able to see the queen present at it's usual laying chamber or the lack of new larva and eggs in cells. The queen's cell, which she is normally found in looks like a peanut hanging off the side or bottom of a comb. If the queen bee died, the remaining bees will choose another potential larva and feed it with extensive amounts of royal jelly. They also build a large hanging cell for the larva. There is nothing to worry about, as long as there is ample larva candidates at the time of the queen's death. The

rest of the colony will automatically fix the problem them selves.

However, there are times where the colony fails and a good beekeeper who does not want to lose the entire colony will need to quickly introduce a new queen to the hive. We discuss how bees can be introduced to a hive later in this book.

Supersedure

This is the state of the colony when the bees are trying to replace their queen, which they consider is failing on her responsibility as a queen. The queen which is probably 2-3 years of age is not laying enough fertile eggs nor producing the adequate amount of Queen Mandibular Pheromone (QMP). QMP is a honeybee pheromone produced by the queen bee and given to her attendants to be distributed to the rest of the bees in the colony. This QMP seems to give the bees a sense of security. When the queen bee fails to produce enough of the QMP, it attracts robber bees. Robber bees are bees from other bee colonies that come and steal honey. This book will further discuss the needed actions taken to prevent such behaviour occurring later in the book.

Swarming

Swarming is when a queen bee leaves a colony, bringing with her about sixty percent of worker bees to form a new colony. This is not to be mistaken with the original queen bee, but the new queen bees that have hatched from its cell. In some cases, worker bees will leave the colony with an un-hatched queen bee.

During the process of swarming, the bees will congregate near the original hive location, some 20 -30 metres away before moving to a permanent nest site. This transitional period is for scout bees to find a new location while all the other bees wait for their signal. This behaviour during a swarm allows beekeepers to effectively retrieve a swarm back to its original hive by simply preventing the queen's ability to fly.

The inability to fly makes the other bees unable to congregate far, and instead end up congregating right outside the hive instead, stopping the whole swarm process. You can easily prevent a queen bee from flying by clipping one of its wings. However, this does not do anything in the case of a swarm with an un-hatched queen bee pupa, and so some occurrences of swarming are unpreventable.

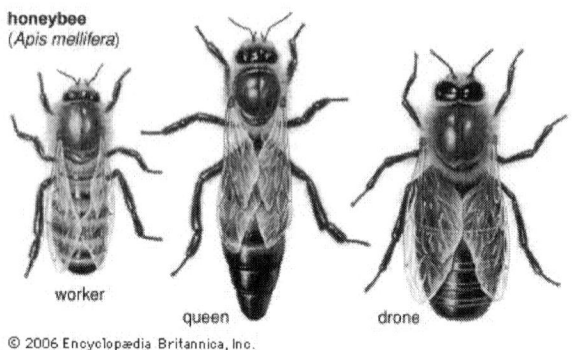

Drone Bees

Drones come from unfertilized eggs. The colony raises drones to mate with the queen when needed but there are no other verified facts about their other purposes aside from this. It is also interesting to note that only 1-2 get to mate with the queen out of the 10,000 drones raised in a year. When there is a shortage of food, drones are removed from the colony and left to die of hunger and cold.

A few days after they come out from their eggs, drones beg for food from the nurse bees and eat from the open cells in the brood nest, which serves as their hangout. After a week, they start flying to find their way around. Another 2 weeks and they are regularly flying to what beekeepers called the Drone Congregation Areas (DCAs). These areas are where drones gather together and where the queen goes when she's ready for mating.

If the drone is lucky enough to mate, then he is sure to sacrifice his life as the mating involves the death of a drone bee. The queen stores up the sperm of the drone she mated with in special receptacles and distributes them as she lays her eggs.

Worker Bees

Like the queen bee, the worker bee starts out as a fertilized egg. Both the queen bee and the worker bee are fed with royal jelly but the worker gets less and less of the jelly as it matures. When the worker bee starts to emerge out of its cell, it serves as a nurse bee and attends to younger larvae or open brood. Its responsibility includes cleaning the cells and generating heat for the brood nest.

In the coming days, its task is promoted to feeding the queen bee and other young larvae as their "nurse". Then the nurse bee will undergo several transition periods, tending to different responsibilities which include, making honey from nectar gathered by other worker bees in the field, building combs, ventilating, guarding and cleaning the bee hive. Worker bees serve as house bees until they are old enough to venture out and become "foragers". Worker bees usually live for a maximum of six weeks except during the winter. They work themselves to death serving the colony.

In case the queen bee fails to perform the responsibility assigned to her in the colony, a worker bee may develop an ovary and starts to lay eggs but usually, these are drone eggs and are found in the worker cell.

CHOOSING THE RIGHT BEE FOR YOU

Beekeepers are faced with the hard decision of choosing which strain or race of honeybee to order and where to obtain the type they have chosen.

Honeybees in the United State, particularly North America are a heterogeneous mixture of several races introduced from Europe, Africa, the Middle East and Asia. The most popular of these various breeds are the Italians, Caucasians, and Carnolians. However, most of these breeds are no longer like the original races they were named after. Strains of these original races were developed through interbreeding and selection along with the influences of the climate and geographic location.

To know which among these strains of bees is suitable for your operation, you need to weigh their advantages and disadvantages. You may try queens and packages from different breeders and suppliers to learn more about their behavior and productivity under your local condition. We always advice new beekeepers to order their first set of bees from a reputable supplier to ensure your colony will be disease free and healthy.

Italian Bees

Of the three breeds mentioned here, the Italian bee seems to be the most popular not only in the United States but in the whole of North America. Since it was introduced in 1959, they have replaced the then commonly found original black German bees brought by the early colonists.

The Italian bee appears to be light yellow or brown with alternate stripes of black and brown on the abdomen. The worker bees that carry three bands on their abdomen are called "leather-colored Italian" while those with five bands are the "goldens" or "cordovan queens".

This breed of bees starts their brood rearing in the early spring until late fall, resulting in a great population during their entire active season. With the large colony, they are able to collect plenty of nectar in a short amount of time. Nonetheless, compared to dark races, they tend to consume honey more during fall or winter, meaning they will require more reserves to survive the winter months. This needs to be noted during your harvesting period.

The Italian bee is gentle and quiet on the combs, making harvesting and handling comparatively easier, but one disadvantage of this strain is their weaker orientation compared to other races. This strain tends to develop more bees that drift from one colony to another and a strong inclination to rob, a strong potential cause of spreading diseases.

The Italians are good housekeepers and are resistant to European foulbrood (EFB). This is the major reason why they are chosen over black bees. They also produce brilliant white cappings ideal for producing comb honey. With the queen's lighter coloring compared to other bees in the colony, you can easily spot her compared to the other two races we mention here.

Caucasian Bees

This breed is the gentlest of all honeybee breeds. You can easily identify them through their dark color with gray bands on their abdomens. They love to build burr comb and use a large quantity of propolis to fasten combs and reduce the size of the entrance. However, there are some new strains that use less propolis as they are producing propolis, making them suitable for producing comb honey.

This breed is also inclined to rob and drift but not

too much on swarming, and they are quite conservative in using their honey better than the Italian breed. Normally, colonies do not reach full strength before midsummer, making the size of a Caucasian bee colony smaller. Caucasian bees also forage at lower temperatures and under less favorable climate compared to the Italian bees. This makes them better suited if you live in areas with cool springs and summers that do not reach a high temperature. They are also resistant to EFB. Though Caucasians are available, they are to find.

Carniolan Bees

Carnoilan bees are dark bees and though they look similar to Caucasians, you can identify them through their brown spots and bands on their abdomens. Over winter, these bees form a smaller cluster and in the spring, when pollen becomes available they increase rapidly which can also result to excessive swarming. During the winter season, they are economical, and easy to maintain as they consume less honey even under unfavourable conditions. They are also quiet in their comb.

Carniolan bees do not tend to rob and have a good sense of orientation. They are also available but not common.

THE BEEHIVE

There are three types of beehives that the most commonly used in the United States of America—the Horizontal Top Bar Hive, the Warre Hive and the Langstroth Hive. Each design caters to the specific needs of a beekeeper.

Types of Beehives

The Horizontal Top Bar Hive comes on top of the popularity list because of its simplicity, accessibility, and lightness. Beginners in beekeeping find this type more appealing since there are only a few required accessories in handling this hive. This type is the most frequently maintained and monitored and requires no heavy lifting involved during the upkeep rounds.

The Warre Hive appeals to beekeepers who simply want to have a hive with light boxes, few accessories and is simple to manage. You can put the boxes to the bottom of the hive in spring and make your harvest in fall. Of the three types here, it has the lowest maintenance requirements.

The Langstroth is the most popular hive type in Northern America. It comes with quite a number of accessories, durable boxes, and available resources; hence, is more appealing to beekeepers that mass-produce. If you want colony growth and huge production of honey, you can add more boxes. This type also requires little maintenance.

Now when it comes to the question, "Which one is the best?", that might be a little bit complicated. You see each of the above mentioned beehives has their own advantages and disadvantages depending on what you need or want to do. For instance, you may want to harvest lots of honey or a little honey. You may even want to consider the bee population or pollination potential in your surrounding area.

It is then imperative for you to know first what you aim to do or know the specifications of the beehive you need. To help you with this, we list down the description, pros, and cons, as well as other details of each beehive type.

Horizontal Top Bar Hive

Also known as the top bar hive, the horizontal top bar hive is said to be the oldest design of the three hive types.

Description:

In this design, a long aperture is installed with wooden bars laid across the top, shoving against each other, sitting side by side. The bees build their honeycombs at the lowest point of the bars, filling up the cavity in the process. As a result, the combs are arranged in a manner akin to bread slices. In terms of weight, it is the lightest (since it has no store boxes or frames), with the involved lifting of 3 to 7 pounds of combs.

Cost:

Ranges from very cheap if you build your very own to moderately expensive when you accessorize it with bells, whistles, and other paraphernalia, or if you choose to buy ready made ones from a supplier.

Production and Colony Health:

Some of the experts say top bar beekeepers can harvest the same honey quantities as their Langstroth hives; even though frequent monitoring and maintenance is required in the process. However, one quality of the top bar hive design is the lack of a foundation for the combs, which boost the health of the bee colony by replicating how natural bee comb is shaped.

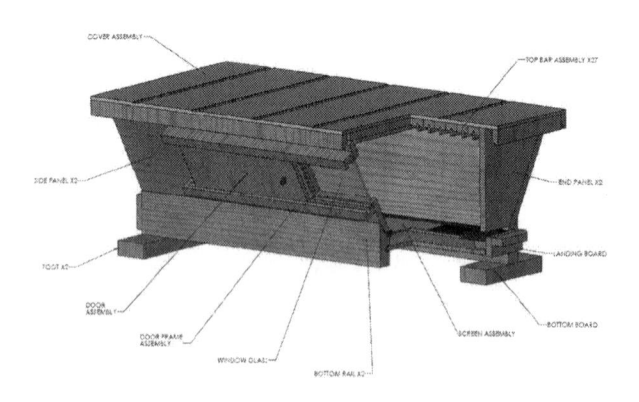

Warre Hive

The Warre hive is named after its designer, Emile Warre; a pragmatic French monk from the 1900's. The design of this hive has not changed at all since it's conception, which proves it's effectiveness.

Description:

Usually, the design starts with two boxes and a package or swarm of bees. It involves stacked boxes along with eight top bars (just like in the horizontal top bar hive), spread evenly across the top of each box. From these bars, the bees build their honeycombs. Furthermore, the boxes of Warre hive are distinctly smaller than those of the Langstroth, having dimensions of 12 square inches versus 19 by 14 inches of the latter.

Cost:

Depending if you will be building your own or buying Warre hive, the cost ranges from low to high. Obviously, the fewer boxes involved, the more you save money.

Production and Colony Health:

Its production can be comparable to that of

Langstroth's if you add the boxes right on time. In terms of colony health, the Warre hive design is the least intrusive towards the bee's natural behaviour. This is because, the boxes are added at the bottom of the hive, where the bees tend to build their colonies in a downward fashion. They are able to manage all of their honey stores to the top boxes and generate a natural cycle of comb removal. Thus, this method promotes health to the bee colony.

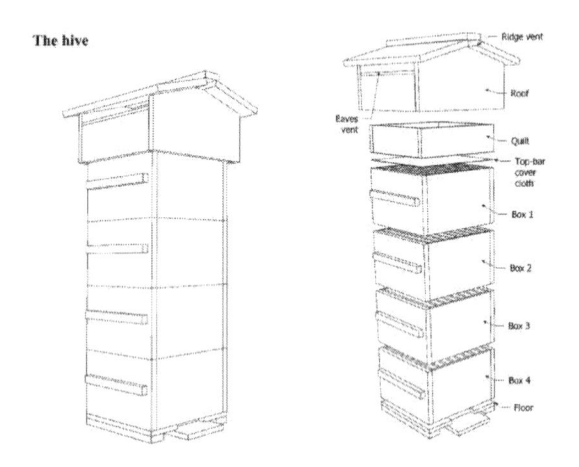

The hive

Langstroth Hive

As mentioned before, this type is the most common in North America as well as Australia. It was invented in the mid-1800 by Lorenzo Langstroth. The most notable feature of this hive is the movable frame. By this, the Langstroth became the most favorite beehive design in modern beekeeping.

Description:

Langstroth consists of several stacked boxes of different heights—shallow, medium and deep. The shallows are the shortest; whereas the deeps are the tallest boxes. It is the heaviest of the three beehive types we have in this discussion. It can weigh from estimated 30 to 80 pounds, depending on the size of the boxes used. Most of the Langstroth beekeepers begin to assemble their hives using either 3 mediums or 2 deep boxes.

Cost:

By comparison, mass produced hives are cheap but component add-ons as well as required accessories are unquestionably costly.

Production and Colony Health:

It has the highest honey production potential of the three due to the size of the boxes. In contrast with Warre, the boxes here are added to the top, a method called "supering." The bees are then encouraged to build their honeycombs in an upward movement. After the bee colony has filled up what they call as the "supers", the beekeepers can then gather the surplus honey supers, allowing the remaining for the colony. Even with combs without a foundation, the chances of survival and healthy existence are just the same as in the top bar and Warre hives.

This hive is best for commercial use as the production of honey is greater, however in recent times this beehive design has come under a fair bit of scrutiny for it's harsh practices within it's commercial use.

Don't forget to leave a review for this book on Amazon if you found this book helpful.

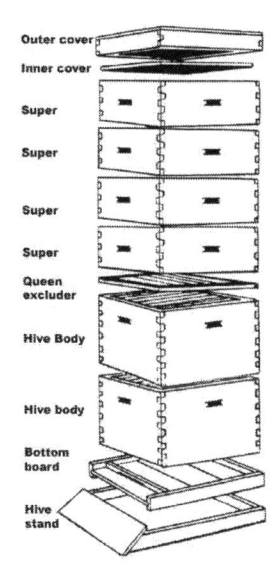

GETTING YOUR BEES INTO THE HIVE

When you are still starting out with your beekeeping adventures, you may worry about where you are going to get your bees. Well, there are four sources where you can obtain them: Package bees, nucs, swarms, and established colonies

Package Bees

This is the most common way for a new beekeeper to start. You can always purchase a package of bees consisting of 3 lbs. of young bees and a mated queen bee. Package bees are obtainable in southern states like Georgia, Texas, and Florida since bee colonies in the South are far ahead in terms of quantity and population than in the Northern states.

These packaged bees are taken from strong colonies and shaken into screened containers. A young mated queen is then added and with a small can of syrup to feed them on the trip to their destination, which hopefully is your doorstep. Since production is usually not enough to meet the demand, package bees are usually sold out. So you need to place your order as early as January or February. It is also important to note that there is no inventory of package bees in the north. Package bees can't be put on "hold" for more than a day.

In Pennsylvania, packages are available in the middle of April when local pollen and nectar are abundant. Packages can take advantage of the condition and develop strong colonies, provided that the queen bee sent with the package is accepted by the worker bees. However, this late delivery can lose you bee population potential as you are starting late into the season.

Nucs

Nucs is actually a coined term from the nucleus,

which is defined as a central or essential core in which other parts around it are assembled. In beekeeping, a nuc is usually 3-5 frames of bees, which consist of a laying queen bee, young bee workers, brood (larvae and pupae), some honey and pollens. It's a great way to get started when you are new to beekeeping, but can be very expensive.

With an established queen bee, you can expect a great population of bees to emerge from a nuc. However, unlike the packages, nucs don't ship well. They are perfect for local production and are available in Pennsylvania until May. Nucs cost a bit more than the package but is usually worth its value if they are shipped properly. However, they are hard to find. Note, that although nucs are great at starting your colony fast, there is potential for serious bee diseases, such as the American Foulbrood.

Established Colonies

Buying this kind has a great advantage as you will have a working colony ready to produce honey. The standard colony can consist of two deep brood boxes, which you could even split into two by adding another queen and you have two great colonies to start with. However, this can also carry hidden pitfalls and risks that include the following:

- Heavy hauling
- Potential for American Foulbrood disease
- Assume risk for over-wintering that colony when you purchase late in summer. (usually around 30% don't survive the winter)

Hence, when you are faced with an opportunity to acquire an established colony of bees, here are some tips to follow:

- Take with you an experienced beekeeper as you inspect the colony of bees.
- Watch out for non-standard equipment, signs of American foulbrood, overall health of the colony and laying queen plus a good brood pattern.
- Make sure that someone with bee movement experience is part of the operation.

- There must be some special precautions to prevent bee leakage and keep them from overheating.

Installing the Bees into the Hives

When you are a beginner, waiting for the delivery of the package of bees you ordered can be scary, exciting and overall an emotional rollercoaster, but any emotion is ok, what is important is that you properly prepare for your bees' arrival. This preparation will ensure

Before the arrival of your bees, you need to set up the place and ready all the equipment. For a minimum, you need the following, this is regardless of which bee hive style you choose to use:

- Hive stand
- 1 Hive body
- Bottom board
- Inner cover
- Outer cover

- 10 or 8 frames with foundation or comb. You can also use foundationless frames.
- Entrance reducer
- Feeder

Note: Boardman feeders are great for package installs, because you can replace the feed without disturbing the settled bees. However, you will find that the reducer will not fit when the feeder is placed. So either you will need a smaller one or make use of a piece of wood to reduce the entrance to the hive to protect it from robbers.

Pick up your bees as soon as your package arrives. Check if the bees as still alive. A pile of dead bees is no good to you, so inform the supplier as soon as possible regarding the condition. You also need to install the bees to their hive right after their arrival. If you can't do it within the day and you need a day or two before properly installing them, be sure you place them in a dark, cool place, which is draft free like your garage or basement.

Using a spray with a 1:1 ratio of water and sugar, feed the bees and lightly mist the outside of the package. Be sure to check and see to it that the spray you will be using has not been used with any pesticides, cleaning solution, etc before.

Sugar solution must be one part warm water and one part white sugar cane sugar. Make enough to feed your bees. You will also need the following:

- A hive tool
- A lit smoker
- A bee suit/veil
- Smoker fuel and lighter
- Duct tape
- A bee brush or feather
- Rim board or rubber bands
- Duct tape (just in case)
- A pocket knife

Late afternoon is the best time for installing the bees into their new hive. When you do this, make sure that the smoker is well lit. This is not really needed but it is a good habit to have when you start inspecting your bees. As an added option, you can mist the outside of the package very lightly with the sugar mixture, if it is above 60 degrees Fahrenheit. This prevents the bees from flying around.

However, don't do this when it is cold outside, as the extra moisture will lower the immediate temperature even further.

Open the package using the hive tool and then dislodge the bees by bumping the package against the ground. Remove the feeder jar and hold the tab of the queen's cage, but don't release.

Remove the queen's cage from the package of bees and replace the lid of the package so the bees won't be able to escape. Open the hive and remove 3-4 frames from one side of the bee hive. If bees cluster to the queen's cage, brush them into the hive using the bee brush or feather, then inspect the queen bee.

It is important to make sure that the queen bee is alive and healthy. Watch her as she walks. Check if she is not gimpy and make sure that all her legs are intact. If the queen bee is dead or injured, get her back into the package, close it, and store in a cool, dark place. Call your supplier as soon as possible for a possible replacement.

Some queen's cages have corks on its two ends. Using your knife, remove only the one from the

CANDY END of the cage.

3 Different Ways to Install the Queen

We have her three different ways to install the queen bee. You can pick any one to use.

Rubber Band Method – You place a rubber band around one frame in the beehive. Then place the cage between the rubber band and the foundation.

Rim Board Method – You place the queen's cage on top of the frames, facing upward, and then place a rim board around her.

Push-In Method – If you are using a drawn comb, push the queen's cage into the wax, sticking it to the comb.

Rubber Band Method

While using the rubber band to hold the queen's cage in place, make sure it is a few inches down so the worker bees can have room to take care and feed her. You may also choose to install the cage vertically behind the rubber band. However, if you choose to do this, make sure that the candy end where you had previously removed the cork is facing up. This way, if some of the worker bees died, they will not fall down into the hole and block the entrance of the queen. Replace the frame while the queen's cage is attached to the middle of the hive. Also, make sure that the queen is always tight there in the center of the hive.

Rim Board Method

In installing the queen bee using the Rim Board Method, hanging the cage is not necessary. Right after removing the cork from the queen's cage, slowly lay the queen's cage on the top bars in the center of the hive. After you had shaken the rest of the bees into the hive and replaced the frames, place a rim board on the hive. This will give the bees space to cluster around their queen.

Push-In Method

This is the perfect method if you have the drawn comb and it is warm outside. Using this method, all you have to do is simply remove the cork from the candy end of the cage and push the queen's cage to the comb in the middle of the frame in the centre of the beehive. The candy cane end must be accessible and be a few inches from the top of the frame.

Also, make sure that the screen can be easily accessible by the worker bees so they can feed their queen bee. Try to face the candy end up so that if ever an attendant bee dies, he won't be blocking the entrance to the queen's cage. After the cage is quite securely in place, gently place one frame against another frame with the cage, closing it as best as it allows.

Installing the Worker Bees

Shake a few cups containing the bees on top of the queen. Notice that these bees will stick their butts in the air. This is to release the "*nasonov pheromone*" to tell other bees that the queen is here. Shake the rest of the worker bees into the space in the beehive where you removed the frames. Try to put in as many bees as you can. Don't worry if you don't get all the bees out as the other bees will just find their way into the hive. After doing these procedures, gently replace the frames. However, don't push the frames on top of the bees, but instead let them fall into place so you don't squeeze the bees in the hive.

Feeding the Bees

Sometimes package bees on the foundation are not provided with food: honey, pollen, or bees bread and they die. By feeding them with the 1:1 sugar solution, you can encourage then to produce beeswax, which they use in building their home and storage or warehouse for their food.

The Boardman feeder is best for this since you don't need to disturb the bees just to see if they have enough food inside. Make sure to keep the feeder full at all times until they have at least 10 frames drawn out or as needed. Be sure not to over feed them during a nectar flow.

Post Installation

After the package is installed, do not touch the hive for at least a week. This is the hardest but an essential part of your beekeeping. Disturbing the bees too much can motivate them to kill their queen bee instead of accepting her. Check if the feeder is full as it is essential to keep the bees well fed.

Since bees are new to their surroundings, they will be flying everywhere. This is part of their orientation flight process, and this can take a few days before they will settle down. Look out for bees that are carrying dead bees. They are the undertaker bees. This is a sign that the colony is doing well. Look also for bees bringing in pollen attached to their legs. They need this pollen to feed the brood. This is a sign that you will have a laying queen bee soon enough.

A Week Later, complete with your safety suit gear; smoke the bees with a puff in the entrance and under the cover. Inspect the queen's cage and see if the queen has been released. If she had, then it's time to remove the queen's cage. But if you find out that the queen has not been released, check to see if she is still alive, put the cage back and then close the hive. After a few days, check the status of the colony again.

MAINTAINING YOUR COLONY & HIVE

During the beekeeping season, which falls from March to November, you as a beekeeper should perform weekly inspections. Inspection is an integral part of the maintenance management program. Your colony's health depends on your efficiency and effectiveness in this department. Through inspection, you can detect problems like honey robbery, malnutrition and the loss of a queen, as well as the early signs of pest infestations and various diseases. Thus, you can immediately troubleshoot or apply necessary precautions and/or cure.

Remember that temperature also plays a vital part during inspection. Do it only when the temperature is over 57°F. You can remove the top cover when it's cooler but never get the frames out as it may chill and kill the brood. It is best to check during midday as most of them are out foraging, making it easier for you to handle the rest.

What Do You Need to Inspect?

Every time you visit your hive, you learn the very things you need to be aware of. While some of the details vary depending on the time or season of the year, you basically inspect to note the productivity and health of the colony. Here are the most common areas you need to check:

Status of Your Queen Bee

- ✓ Each time you visit your hive, check for the presence of the queen. Is she still there? Is she still alive? Is she still laying eggs?

✓ Since you can't spot her easily, try to locate the eggs. They're much easier to find than their mom during sunny days.

Food Storage and the Brood

For every deep frame or comb, there are approximately 7,000 cells depending on the size of the frame. These cells are used by the bees for food storage and raising brood. Upon inspection, note what's happening with these cells so you can analyze the health and performance of your bees.

Assess the amount of brood in your hive. Bear in mind that the amount of brood in your hive varies all throughout the year. The months of April and May are the peak; June to August is hot and dry so the amount may be less; September signals the preparation for the winter season, hence, there should be a good amount of brood produced during this month; December gives little if ever; and January gradually starts the process.

Brood Pattern

Remember that brood pattern determines the status of your queen. A close-packed brood pattern conveys a healthy queen. On the other hand, a loose or spotted pattern (depicted as something with a lot of empty cells), indicates an old, unhealthy queen. You may need to replace her to ensure the overall health of your colony.

Food Inside the Beehive

Your bees collect various kinds of food, which they store inside their hive. They stockpile pollens, nectar, and water. You will distinguish the pollens as they come in different colors like yellow, orange, gray, brown, blue, etc. Meanwhile, when you see wet cells, then they may contain water or nectar.

Abnormalities

Search for signs of swarming, backfilling, pest infestation and abnormal activities. A strong bee population is good, but swarming is another story. Over populated hives tend to have aggressive bees and that would be a big problem beekeepers like you. Moreover, you must search for signs of mites and beetle larvae, which can be very devastating to your hive's population later.

How Do You Inspect the Hives?

Now that you know what to inspect, let's get down on how to inspect. First, you must be acquainted with the auxiliary tools and equipment.

Smoker

A smoker is made up of a grate and metal fire pot with appending bellows. The most popularly used smoker is the 4x7" but you can choose your own preference. But for safety measures, choose one with a heat shield surrounding the firebox. This helps you and or your clothes from getting burnt.

In order to make big quantities of cool and thick smoke, put the coals on the grate and put the unburned mediums situated above the coals. You can use bark, wood shavings, cardboard, burlap, punk wood, cotton rags, corncobs and dry leaves as smoker fuels. Alternatively, you can use liquid smoke that you can safely spray on your bees.

Hive Tool

It is a metallic bar used for extracting the frames in a honey super or brood chamber. It also helps rub down wax and propolis to divide hive bodies.

Protective Clothing

It is imperative that you wear a bee veil every time you perform the inspection. It protects your face and neck from any possible bee stings. There are three kinds of veils: hatless veils, those that come as part of a bee suit and the ones that can be pulled over a hat.

Bee suits or what we call coveralls, they can be expensive but they are a good investment. They come in various colors although the white or tan are deemed most appropriate when working, other accessories which add another layer of protection are leather gloves or canvass.

Don't forget to protect areas such as your ankle and wrists. Most angry bees attack your ankles since they are at the level of the bees' hive entrance. Use tape as an easy solution to make sure no bees get at your ankles.

Firm Grip

For those who find it uneasy to use their hands to pull out a frame, a frame grip can be a good investment. The downside of using this, however, is that you may crush bees in the process since you cannot feel them while using a firm grip.

Now that you have gotten acquainted with the auxiliary equipment, let's move on to the steps.

1. Start by lighting your smoker and focus the smoke at the entrance (be careful not to over-do it, though).
2. Remove the top of the hive and smoke there, too.
3. Remove the first frame or the wall frame and it doesn't matter which end you choose.
4. Examine the frame and set it aside. Do these steps to all the frames—mind the order, though—and replace them together.
5. Carefully pry the frames apart to create room to return the end frame.
6. Remove the top box with minimal twisting in order for it to loosen up from the frames located in the bottom box.
7. Set the top box aside but do not put it on the ground!
8. Check the bottom box and record your findings.
9. Replace everything but keep in mind that you should never leave spaces in between

frames as the bees tend to fill them up with comb.

How to Render Beeswax

Usually, beekeepers collect beeswax in the form of old combs, crumbs of wax and cappings. Accumulated, these surmount to your significant wax harvest for the whole year. For instance, you were able to harvest 200 pounds of honey. Out of it, you get approximately 4 pounds of wax, which have more worth than that of honey. The wax can be processed and be used to create different kinds of products.

Using Solar Vex-melter
When it comes to rendering, the use of solar vex-melter deems to be an efficient and secure method. This simple device made of wood, glass and metal plates requires little effort and usage, plus it generates premium quality wax.

It has an airtight base, which can generate 61° centigrade during a sunny day, enough to melt a bee comb, making both beeswax and honey. To help it take in more heat, the vex-melter can be painted black.

Using the Hot Bath Method
If you don't have a wax melter, you can use the hot bath method instead. However, this can only be used after crushing the combs and extracting the honey.

What You Need

- 2-3 meter of twine (or string)
- 1 stick (or top bar)
- 1 sack (or sackcloth)
- Cooking pot
- 1 wax mold
- 1 ladle (or large spoon)

Steps

1. Pour water into the cooking pot. The amount should depend on the quantity of the bee combs. Place the cooking pot over the stove.
2. Wash the crushed bee combs to get rid of the dirt and put it inside the sack.
3. Tie up a string or twine around the sack, making it look like a nice-looking parcel.
4. As the water warms, put the parcel into the pot. Using the stick or top-bar, push the parcel to the bottom.
5. Upon reaching 59°C temperature and the wax melts, you can notice that a waxy scum appears at the top. Get this using the ladle or spoon and pour it into the mold. Continue to do this until nothing's surfacing anymore.

Important: You must not subject the wax to high temperature during the procedure. Reduce the heat to avoid boiling the water, you only want melt the wax not burn it or boil it.

How to Collect Honey

In harvesting honey during summer, make sure that you leave enough for the bees just in case there may be scarcity during the autumn harvest. It is a good practice

leaving them a full allocation of honey for them all the time. This assures the health of the colony, by ensuring their food supply.

Harvesting honey in spring and summer at the time before the goldenrod flow begins will allow variations in the honey's taste and flavor. Honey produced in summer has the mild, light taste; whereas, honey produced in fall bears a dark, rich flavor. The latter also can be crystallized quickly and can be a challenge upon the time of extraction if you wait to harvest the entire crop.

Additionally, the fall honey should only be harvested after a killing frost. It is preferable to remove supers and frames when they are completely capped, but three-quarters capped is also acceptable. This is due to the fact that uncapped honey or "green honey" contains a high level of moisture which can generate yeast. It can have a soft and sticky consistency and tastes rather inferior.

In collecting honey, we are going to undergo two processes—the actual harvest and the extraction itself.

Part One: Honey Harvest

What You Need

- Beekeepers suit ensemble (complete with veil and gloves)
- Smoker
- Hive tool
- Frame super

Steps

1. Light the smoker using your choice of fuel.
2. Transfer the frames with honeycomb into the supers. As an alternative, you can also

cover the super with a cloth to avoid bees from going into it.
3. Slowly lift the hive lid using the hive tool and apply smoke.
4. Pull out the frames from the super and examine the honey combs. You can only harvest the frames with capped cells.
5. Bring the super out of the hive and put it in to a clean area. Do this to all the supers if applicable.
6. Just in case that there are additional cells between the frames and supers, you can scrape them off using the hive tool.
7. Get the frames with honey and transfer them into the harvest super.
8. Know that there may be different colors of honey combs on each frame. Light color means pure honey; the darker shade contains pollen, and tan color (usually located right in the middle of the hive) has the capped brood.

Part Two: Honey Extraction

What You Need

- Extractor
- Food-grade bucket
- Double sieve
- Containers
- Tub
- Uncapping fork
- Heated knife

Steps

1. Get the frame of capped honey and put the frame in the tub of honey and wax.
2. Using a heated knife, open the cells, slanting the knife on the frame edges at 30-degree angle. Remember to work fast as the heat may burn the honey. Do this on both sides of the frame.
3. There will be leftover caps and for this, you are going to use the uncapping fork. Just gently scrape off the caps and you're okay.
4. Preheat the extractor and put the uncapped frames into it as you uncap them.

5. When all the frames are done, close the lid and get on with the extractor. The extracting process starts slowly, eventually keeps the pace and finally speeds up. All the honey should be processed in about 10-15 minutes.
6. Put the food-grade bucket right under the extractor faucet to catch the flowing honey. Use the double sieve to strain the impurities and wax.
7. You can transfer the honey into a temporary jug and leave it be for about 12 hours, enough to let the air bubbles disperse.
8. In storing, you should wash first the containers and air-dry them. Fill them up with honey and store.

HOW TO AVOID & SOLVE COMMON PROBLEMS

You will encounter problems along the way in the beekeeping business. While we can enumerate many of them, we have listed the three most common dilemmas that you may encounter from time-to-time. In this chapter, we are going to talk about how to handle these three problems:

- Lost or dead queen bee

- Honey robbery

- Bee pests and probable chemical contamination

Lost or Dead Queen Bee

One of the beekeeper's most dreaded moments is when they lose their colony's queen bee. Her absence means the "death" of the colony once it goes undetected. This is why it is imperative that a beekeeper must check on the queen in every inspection or maintenance schedule.

Oftentimes, beginners in beekeeping panic when they cannot spot the queen immediately. If you're just starting in beekeeping, always remember that she usually dwells inside the hive. If at first you cannot spot her, search for her eggs or young larvae. Their presence means that she is there or that she was there at least days ago.

Now, given the chance that you found out that the colony has lost their queen, what should you do? There are actually two options—either you let the colony naturally replace their lost queen or give them a new one.

Introducing a New Queen

Let's first talk about the latter method we mentioned. Of the two, this is the quicker method, which entails you to order a queen bee from a bee supplier. The advantages of this method include: (1) it is the quickest way to replace the lost queen; (2) the acquired queen is sure to breed, and (3) she breeds a guaranteed pedigree as queens who mate in the wild may breed bees with unpleasant characteristics (e.g. being aggressive).

In introducing the new queen, you must not put her inside the hive instantly. Understand that she's still an outsider and that the other bees will kill her if you just put her there without acquainting her to the colony. To help you with this process, follow these steps:

1. Remove one of the frames. Choose the one with no brood or less brood in it, as these bees will be sacrificed.

2. Eliminate the bees in the frame and do not use it for a whole week.

3. Now that you pulled out one of the frames,

make a gap right in the middle of the brood box. In the space, hang the queen's cage just like how you did it when you first stationed your package bees.

4. Ensure that you bare the candy plug by uncorking the queen's cage. Another reminder, be sure that the end with the candy plug faces upwards so you can avoid the scenario wherein dead attendant bees block the hole where the queen should get out. Check on them after a week to know whether the queen was able to exit from the cage and is already breeding.

Honey Robbery

Honey robbery happens when bees from the other hives attack a hive to steal. The effects of such abnormal activity can be disastrous. First, since there is an attack, there will be lost of lives. In serious cases, the population decline can be drastic to the extent that a whole colony can be wiped out! Another effect will be on the bees' behavior. Those who were attacked can turn to be very nasty and ill-tempered. Ultimately, the invaders take away the food, rendering a hive food-less.

The mistake with most novice beekeepers is that they tend to overlook the "buzzing" crowd as the bees are into their business. As a beekeeper, you should always be observant with the behavior and activities of your bees. You have to know the normal behavior of the bees from the abnormal ones. Here are some clues that there is a honey robbery going on in the hive:

- Robbing bees cannot directly go inside the hive. Hence, they usually do the side-to-side movement, which simply means that they are looking for the opportunity to sneak past through the guards.
- There is combat right at the entrance. These fighting bees are locked in a deathly embrace.
- Foraging bees leave the hive without the honey; whereas, the invaders leave with it. The robbers tend to leave by climbing first upfront of the hive before flying away. Notice that there's a sudden dip once they take off, indicating that they bring their loot with them.

In order to avoid robbery, it is important that you

keep these key points in mind:

- Do not feed your bees out in the open.

- Do not be neglectful by leaving the honey in the open most especially near a bee hive during nectar shortage. This will incite honey robbing.
- Do cover your supers after removing them from the colony during harvest season.
- Do not spill even a tiny drop of sugar syrup during feeding time.

- Do use an entrance reducer in order to limit the opening that your bees must safeguard. Do this method at least until your hive has enough ability to protect itself.

CONCLUSION

Now, that you have come to the end of your reading, you are now sufficiently equipped with the basics of beekeeping and you can start from here.

Little as they are, these bees do play an important role in our lives. Learning all about their sacrifices for nature is enough reason to convince us to raise bees and help them go on with their existence. If we can't help them, then we are not helping ourselves as well. Aside from adding beauty to our surroundings, they help improve our economy while they help our farmers in their production.

I hope this book has enlightened you on the importance of our little friends and your beekeeping journey is long and successful.

Remember to check out my authors' page for my latest works related to homesteading here: www.amazon.com/author/homesteadmike

Please don't hesitate to leave a review on Amazon if you found my book helpful and informative to your beekeeping journey.

ABOUT THE AUTHOR

Michael Moore grew up in the beautiful plains of Colorado all his life with a hardworking farming background. Having his own commercial soy farm, which was passed down from his father. However, Michael wanted to expand his knowledge and skill set from an early age and started rearing cattle and growing other crops on the family farm. Now with over 4 decades of farming experience in both crops and livestock rearing he has built a completely self sufficient small farm for his family of 5. Producing fruit, vegetable, herbs, meat, fish and all natural by-products such as honey, cheese and eggs all throughout the year.

Michael believes everyone anywhere can enjoy the benefits of becoming self-sufficient, and plans to write a series of books aimed at various levels of expertise to help individuals on their own homesteading journey.

Printed in Great Britain
by Amazon